Music Minus One Alto or Tenor Sax
and other B♭ or E♭ Instruments

Glenn Zottola

a tribute to Charlie Parker

Music Minus One Alto or Tenor Sax
and other B♭ or E♭ Instruments

12223

Glenn Zottola

a tribute to Charlie Parker

CONTENTS

SOLO Eb ALTO SAXOPHONE

Moonlight in Vermont

Karl Suessdorf and John Blackburn

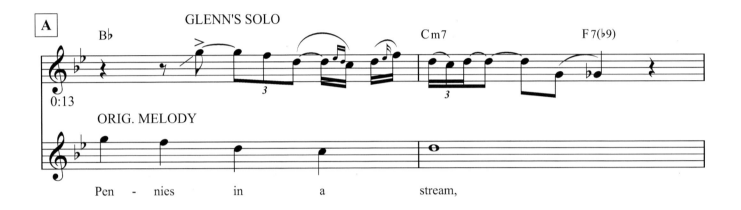

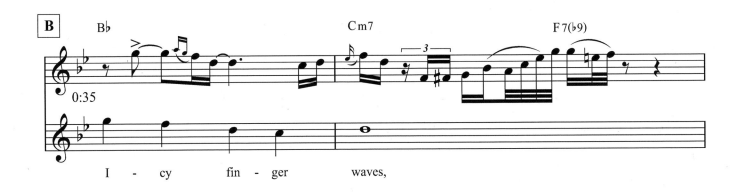

I - cy fin - ger waves,

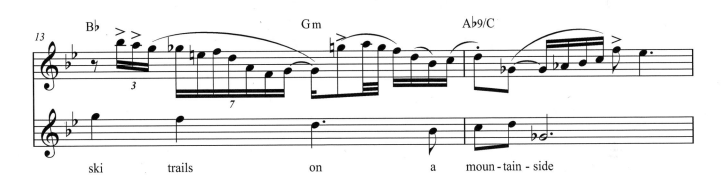

ski trails on a moun - tain - side

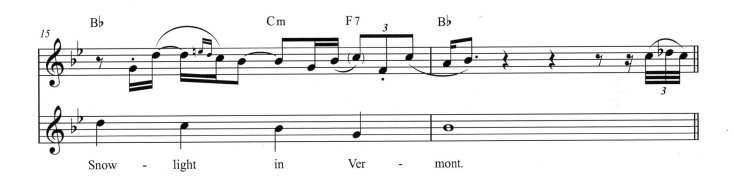

Snow - light in Ver - mont.

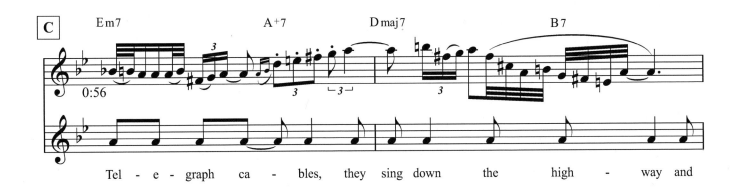

Tel - e - graph ca - bles, they sing down the high - way and

6

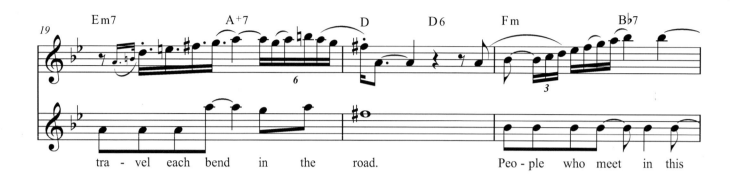

tra - vel each bend in the road. Peo - ple who meet in this

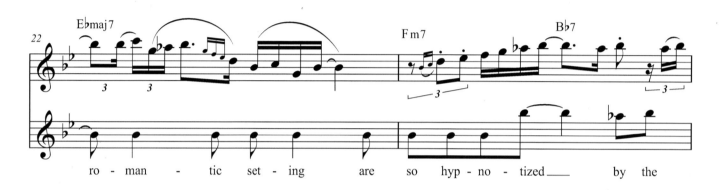

ro - man - tic set - ing are so hyp - no - tized____ by the

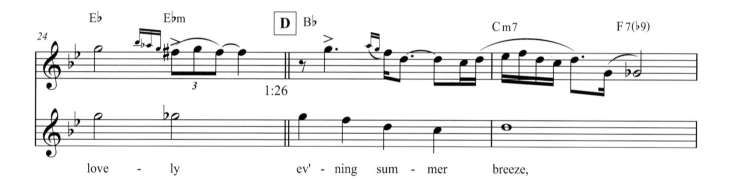

love - ly ev' - ning sum - mer breeze,

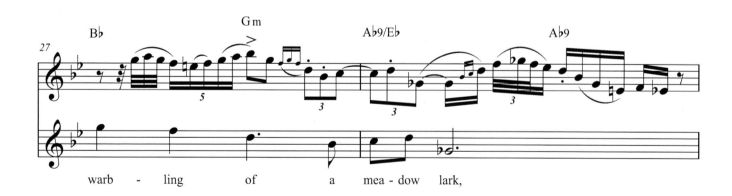

warb - ling of a mea - dow lark,

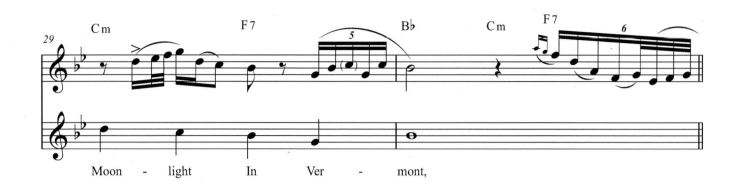

Moon - light In Ver - mont,

E

1:48

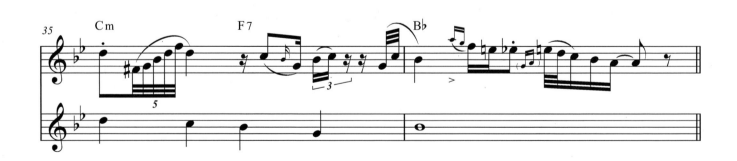

8

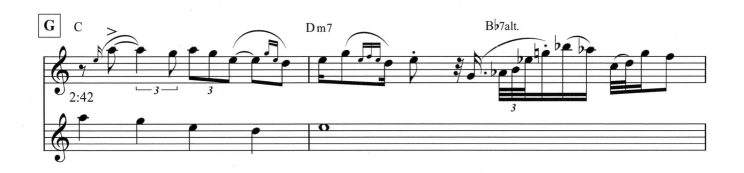

Eb ALTO SAXOPHONE

Oh Lady Be Good

George and Ira Gershwin

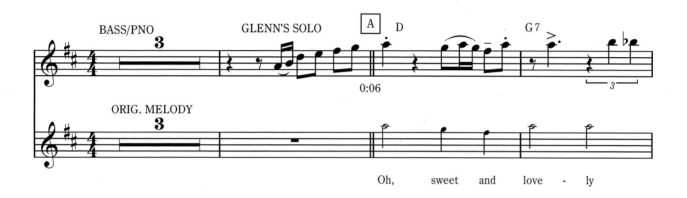

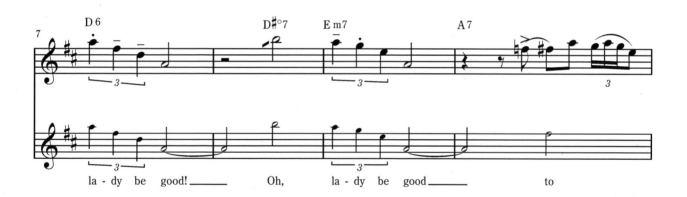

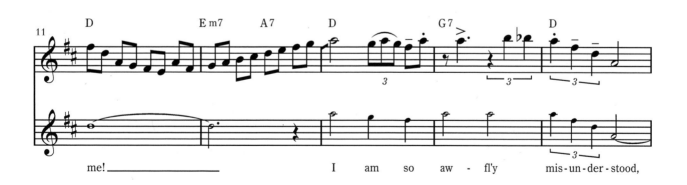

MMO 12223

so la - dy be good_____ to

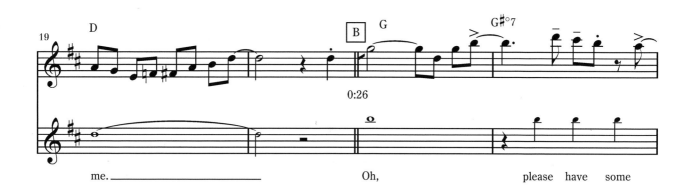

me._____ Oh, please have some

pi - ty,_____ I'm all a - lone in this big

cit - y, I tell you I'm just a lone - some

babe in the wood,_____ so la - dy be good_____ to

me!_____

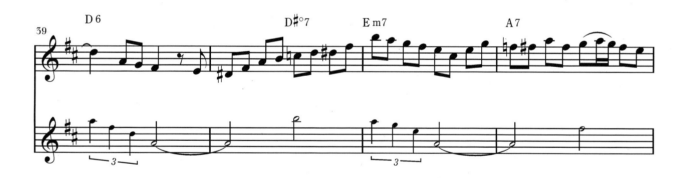

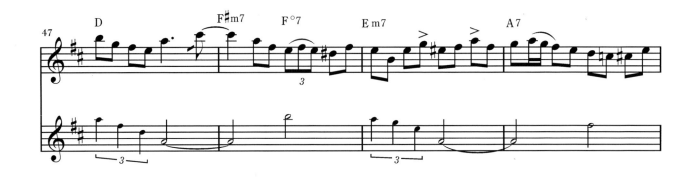

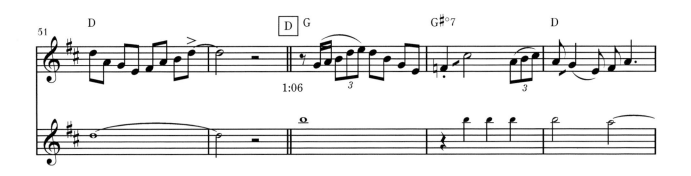

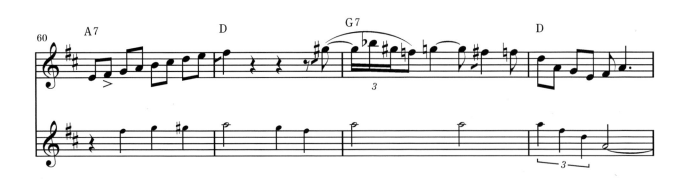

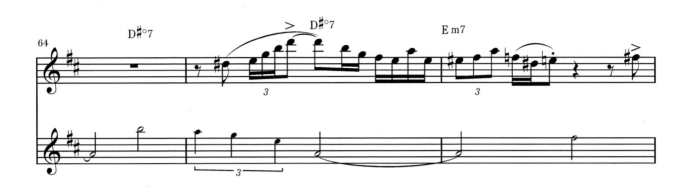

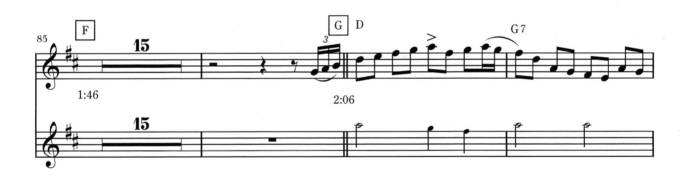

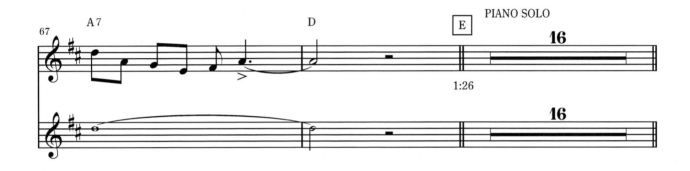

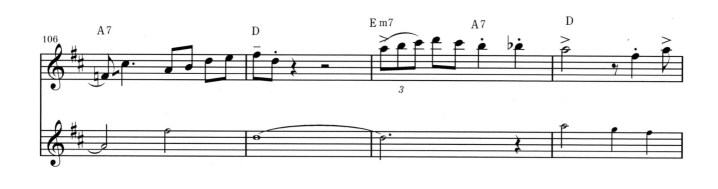

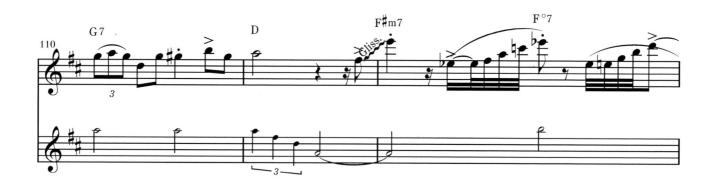

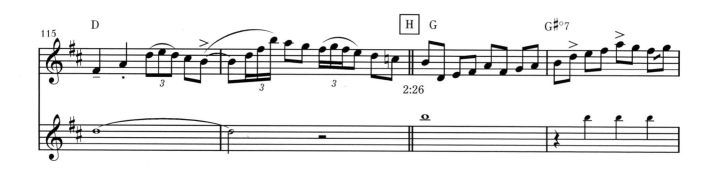

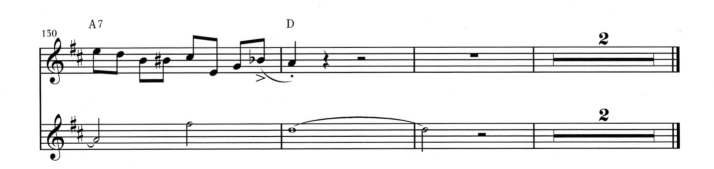

SOLO E♭ ALTO SAXOPHONE

It Might As Well Be Spring

from State Fair
Lyrics by Oscar Hammerstein II
Music by Richard Rodgers

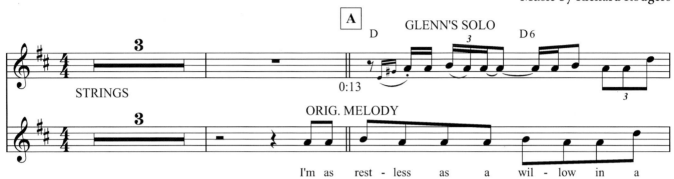

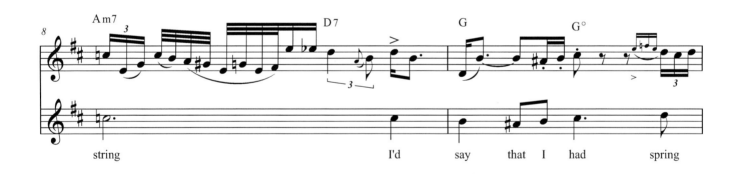

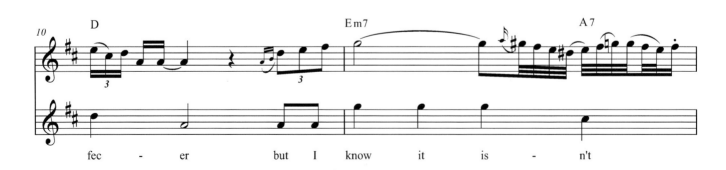

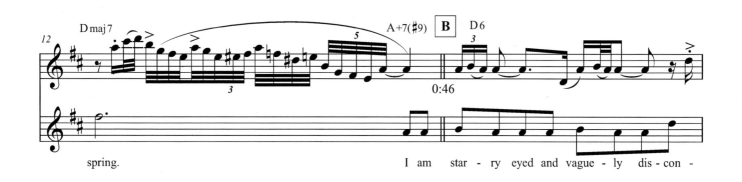

spring.   I am star - ry eyed and vague - ly dis - con -

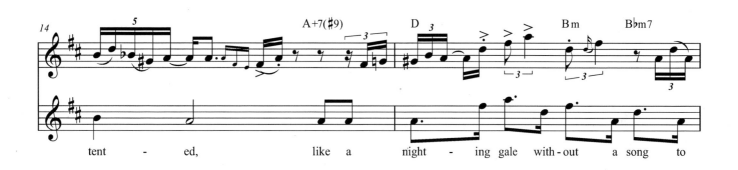

tent - ed,   like a   night - ing gale with - out a song to

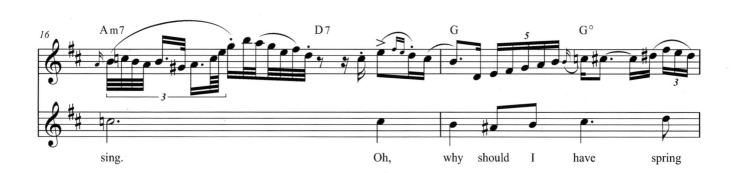

sing.   Oh,   why should I   have spring

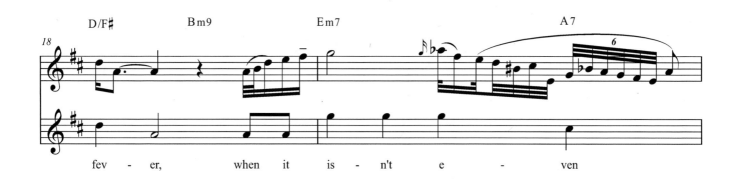

fev - er,   when it is - n't e - ven

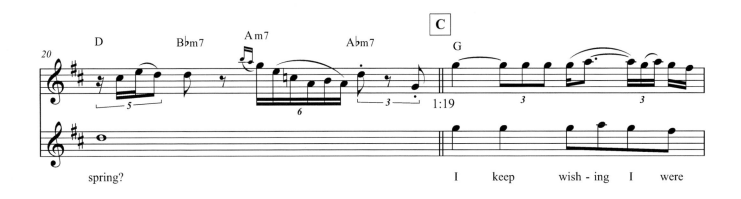

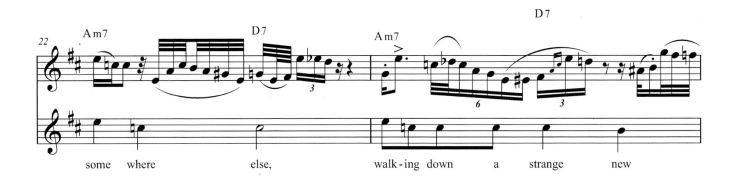

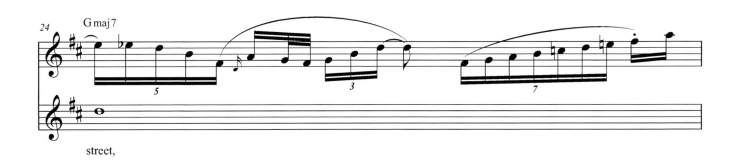

man I've yet to

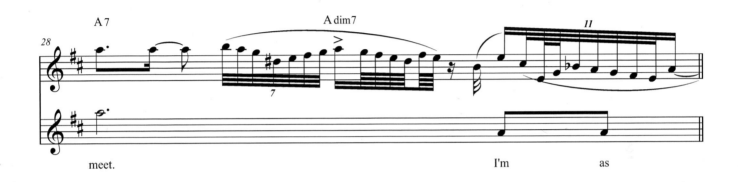

meet. I'm as

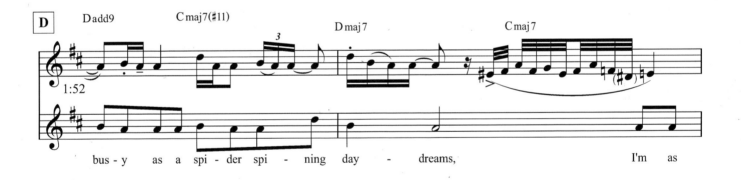

bus - y as a spi - der spi - ning day - dreams, I'm as

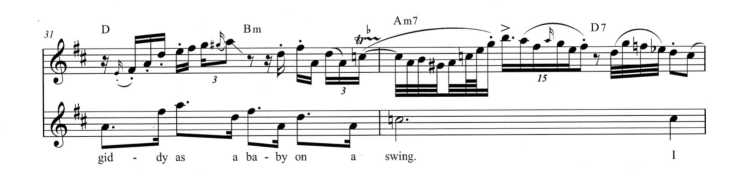

gid - dy as a ba - by on a swing. I

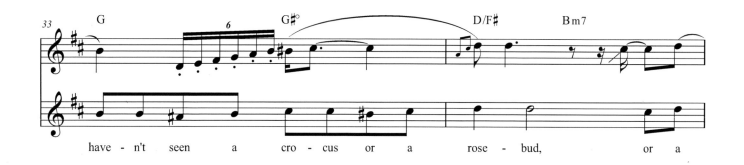

have - n't seen a cro - cus or a rose - bud, or a

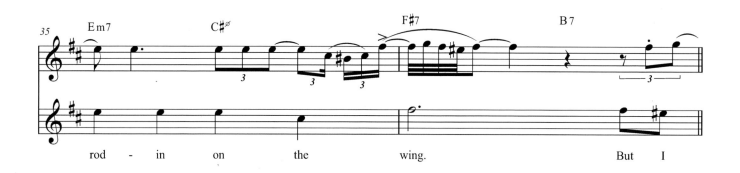

rod - in on the wing. But I

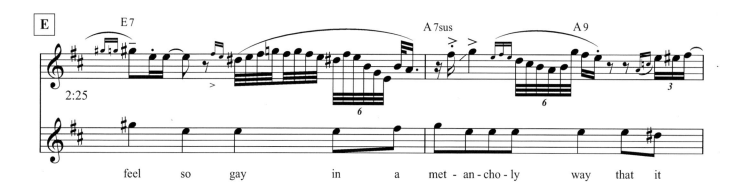

feel so gay in a mel - an - cho - ly way that it

might as well be spring. It

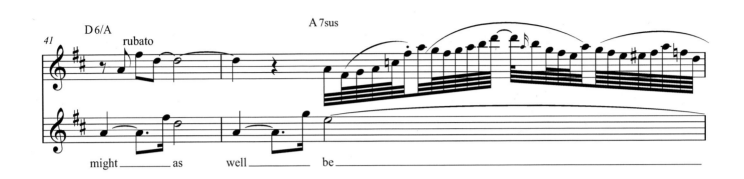

might _____ as well _____ be _____

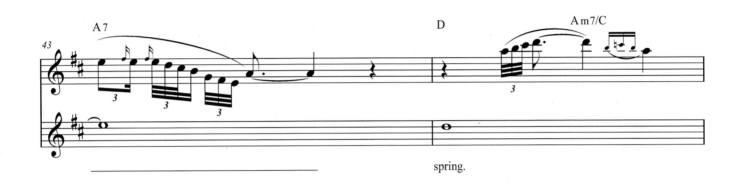

_____ spring.

SOLO Eb ALTO SAXOPHONE

In The Wee Small Hours of the Morning

Lyrics by Bob Hilliard
Music by David Mann

dusk   till   dawn   as   the   clock   tichs   on,

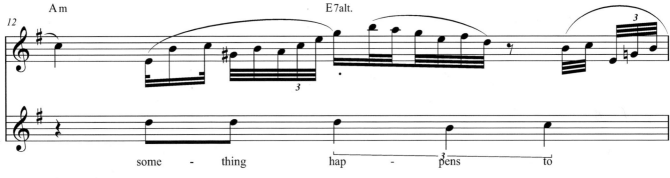

some - thing   hap - pens   to

you. _____   In the

wee   small   hours   of   the   morn - ing, _____   while the

0:56

whole wide world is fast a - sleep, you

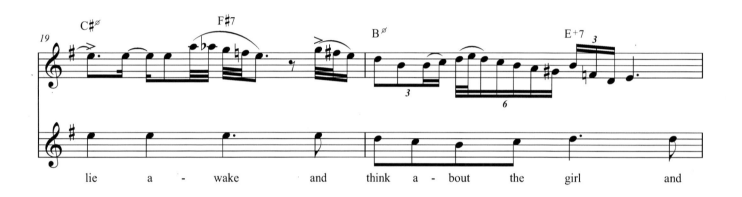

lie a - wake and think a - bout the girl and

nev - er, e - ver think of count - ing sheep. When your

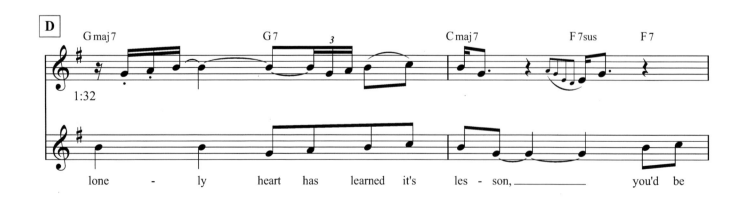

lone - ly heart has learned it's les - son, you'd be

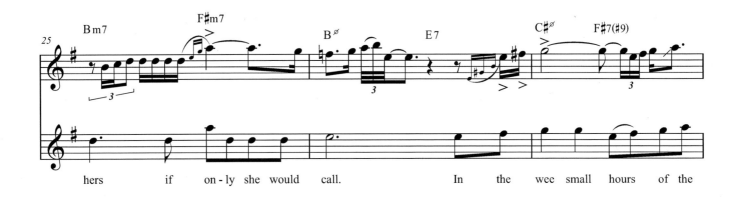

hers   if   on - ly   she   would   call.   In   the   wee   small   hours   of   the

morn - ing, ___   that's   the   time   you   miss   her   most   of

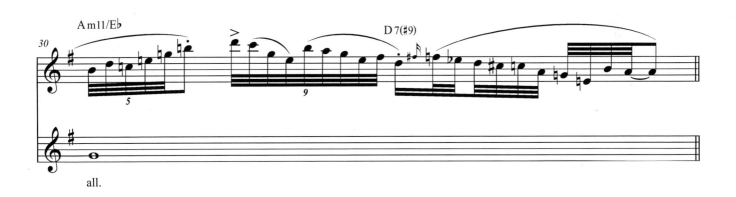

all.

MMO 12223

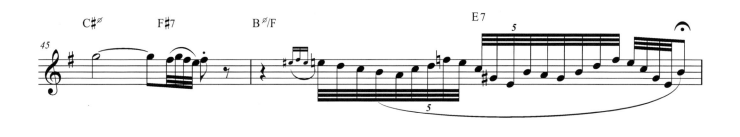

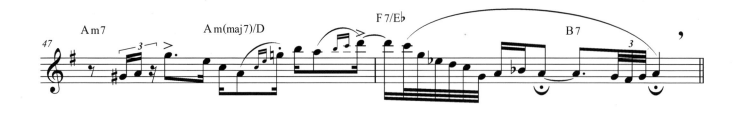

SOLO Eb ALTO SAXOPHONE

What Is This Thing Called Love

Cole Porter

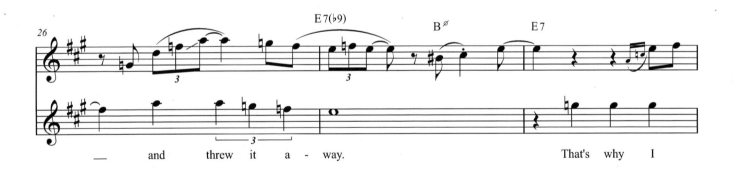

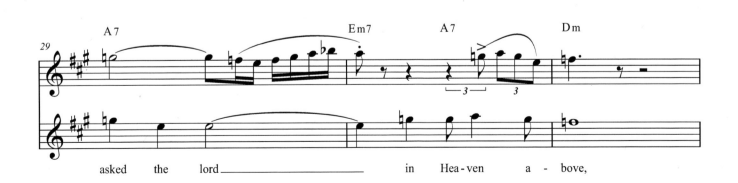

What is this thing＿＿＿＿ called love?

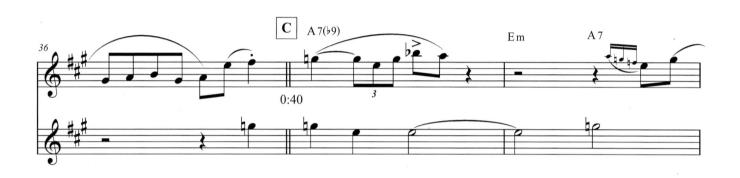

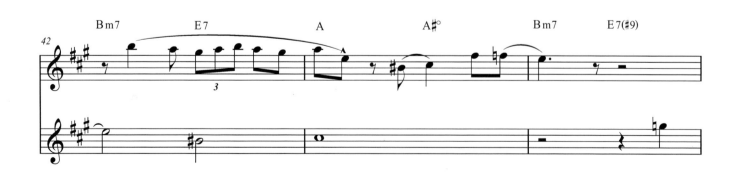

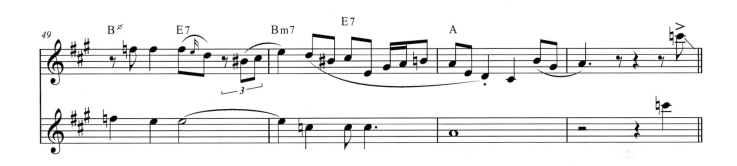

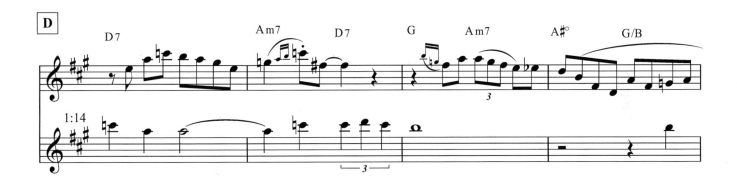

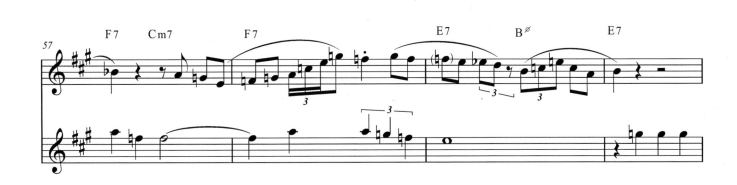

34

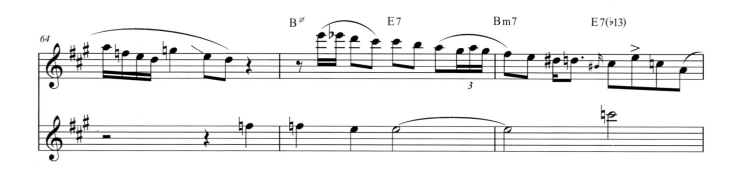

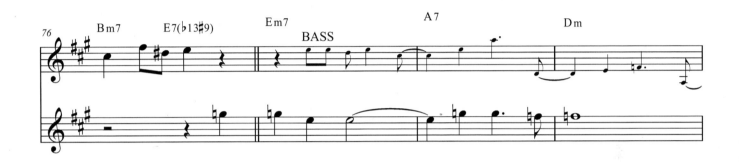

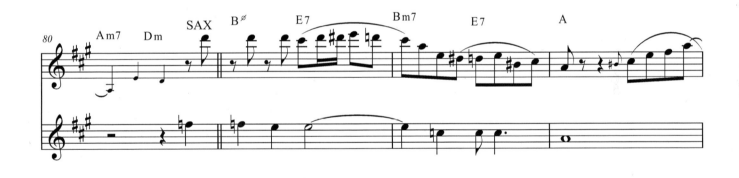

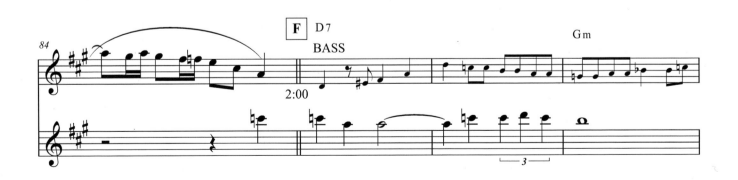

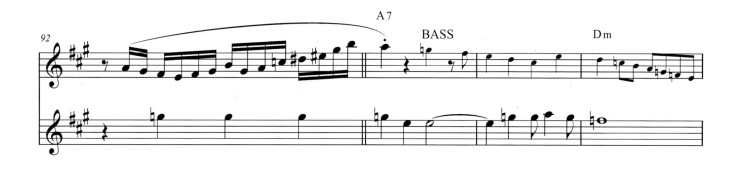

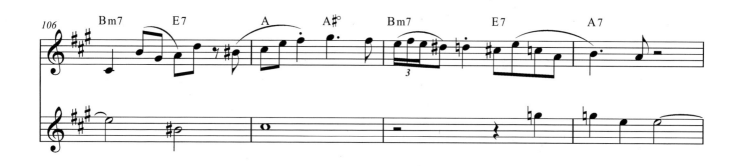

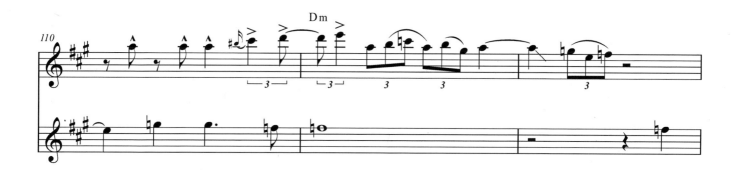

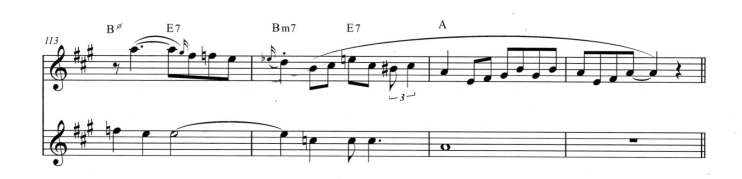

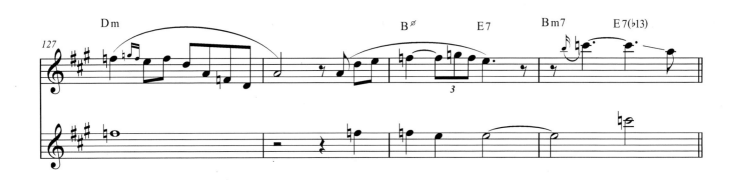

Music Minus One
DISTINGUISHED ACCOMPANIMENT EDITIONS

Saxophone (alto)

Chamber Classics
____ Music for Sax Quartet ....MMO CD 4128 $29.98

Folk, Bluegrass and Country
____ Boots Randolph, vol. 2: Embraceable Tunes.....................MMO CD 4276 $24.98
____ Boots Randolph: Nashville Classics ....MMO CD 4223 $24.98
____ Boots Randolph: Some Favorite Songs - Stds w/Band......MMO CD 4275 $24.98

Inspirational Classics
____ Boots Randolph: When the Spirit Moves You...................MMO CD 4222 $24.98
____ Christmas Memories ....MMO CDG 1203 $19.98

Instrumental Classics with Orchestra
____ Band Aids: Concert Band Favorites ....MMO CD 4127 $29.98
____ GLAZUNOV & VON KOCH Concerti......................MMO CD 4132 $39.98
____ Popular Concert Favorites w/Orch ....MMO CD 4126 $24.98

Jazz, Standards and Big Band
____ 2+2=5: A Study Odd Times.......................MMO CD 2041 $19.98
____ Bacharach Revisited ....MMO CD 4224 $24.98
____ Back to Basics in the Style of the Basie Band ....MMO CD 4277 $19.98
____ Bluesaxe: Blues for Sax ....MMO CD 4205 $19.98
____ Cool Jazz ....MMO CD 4216 $19.98
____ Days of Wine & Roses/Sensual Sax ....MMO CD 4121 $19.98
____ For Saxes Only: Bob Wilber ....MMO CD 4204 $19.98
____ Funkdawgs: Jazz Fusion Unleashed.......................MMO CD 2031 $19.98
____ Jazz Standards w/Rhythm Section ....MMO CD 3218 $29.98
____ Jazz Standards w/Strings ....MMO CD 3219 $29.98
____ Lee Konitz Sax Duets ....MMO CD 4110 $19.98
____ Northern Lights ....MMO CD 2001 $19.98
____ Play Ballads w/a Band ....MMO CD 4105 $19.98
____ Play Lead in a Sax Section: Bob Wilber ....MMO CD 4120 $19.98
____ Sinatra, Sax and Swing ....MMO CD 4217 $19.98
____ Jazz Flute Jam ....MMO CD 3376 $19.98
____ Standards for Tenor Sax, vol. 1 (Glenn Zottola) ....MMO CD 12221 $24.98
____ Standards for Tenor Sax, vol. 2 (Glenn Zottola ....MMO CD 12222 $24.98
____ Studio City ....MMO CD 2021 $19.98
____ Sweet Sixteen Sax Duets (Hal McCusick) ....MMO CD 4235 $19.98
____ Swing with a Band ....MMO CD 4107 $19.98
____ Take One (minus Lead Alto Sax) ....MMO CD 2011 $19.98
____ The Swing Era: Munich Brass ....MMO CD 4122 $19.98
____ Two Much! 16 Tenor Duets for
  Saxophone (Hal McCusick) ....MMO CD 4134 $19.98

Latin Classics
____ JOBIM Brazilian Bossa Novas w/Strings ....MMO CD 4106 $29.98

Laureate Master Series Concert Solos
____ Beginning Solos, v. I (Brodie).......................MMO CD 4111 $19.98
____ Beginning Solos, v. II (Abato) ....MMO CD 4112 $19.98
____ Int. Solos, v. I (Brodie) ....MMO CD 4113 $19.98
____ Int. Solos, v. II (Abato) ....MMO CD 4114 $19.98
____ Advanced Solos, v. I (Brodie) ....MMO CD 4115 $19.98
____ Advanced Solos, v. II (Abato) ....MMO CD 4116 $19.98
____ Advanced Solos, v. III (Brodie) ....MMO CD 4117 $19.98
____ Advanced Solos, v. IV (Abato) ....MMO CD 4118 $19.98

Student Series
____ Solos: Student Ed., v. I.......................MMO CD 4101 $19.98
____ Solos: Student Ed., v. II ....MMO CD 4102 $19.98
____ Classic Themes: 27 Easy Songs ....MMO CD 4130 $19.98
____ Easy Jazz Duets 2 Alto Saxes/Rhythm Section ....MMO CD 4103 $19.98
____ Take a Chorus ....MMO CD 7008 $19.98
____ Teacher's Partner: Basic Studies ....MMO CD 4119 $19.98
____ Twelve Classic Jazz Standards ....MMO CD 7010 $19.98
____ Twelve More Classic Jazz Standards ....MMO CD 7011 $19.98
____ World Favorites:41 Easy Selections.......................MMO CD 4129 $19.98

Saxophone (tenor)

Chamber Classics
____ Music for Sax Quartet ....MMO CD 4211 $29.98

Folk, Bluegrass and Country
____ Boots Randolph, vol. 2: Embraceable Tunes.....................MMO CD 4276 $24.98
____ Boots Randolph: Nashville Classics ....MMO CD 4223 $24.98
____ Boots Randolph: Some Favorite Songs - Stds w/Band......MMO CD 4275 $24.98

Inspirational Classics
____ Boots Randolph: When the Spirit Moves You...................MMO CD 4222 $24.98
____ Christmas Memories ....MMO CDG 1203 $19.98

Instrumental Classics with Orchestra
____ Band Aids: Concert Band Favorites ....MMO CD 4213 $29.98
____ Popular Concert Favorites w/Orch ....MMO CD 4212 $24.98

Jazz, Standards and Big Band
____ 2+2=5: A Study Odd Times.......................MMO CD 2042 $19.98
____ Bacharach Revisited ....MMO CD 4224 $24.98
____ Back to Basics in the Style of the Basie Band ....MMO CD 4277 $19.98
____ Bluesaxe: Blues for Sax ....MMO CD 4205 $19.98
____ Cool Jazz ....MMO CD 4216 $19.98
____ Days of Wine & Roses ....MMO CD 4210 $19.98
____ For Saxes Only: Bob Wilber ....MMO CD 4204 $19.98
____ Funkdawgs: Jazz Fusion Unleashed.......................MMO CD 2031 $19.98
____ Jazz Standards w/Rhythm Section ....MMO CD 3218 $29.98
____ Jazz Standards w/Strings ....MMO CD 3219 $29.98
____ New Orleans Classics ....MMO CD 4221 $19.98
____ Northern Lights ....MMO CD 2002 $19.98
____ Play Ballads w/a Band ....MMO CD 4228 $19.98
____ Play Lead in a Sax Section: Bob Wilber All-Stars ....MMO CD 4209 $19.98
____ Sinatra, Sax and Swing ....MMO CD 4217 $19.98
____ Jazz Flute Jam ....MMO CD 3376 $19.98
____ Standards for Tenor Sax, vol. 1 (Glenn Zottola) ....MMO CD 12221 $24.98
____ Standards for Tenor Sax, vol. 2 (Glenn Zottola) ....MMO CD 12222 $24.98
____ Standards for Trumpet, vol. 1 (Bob Zottola) ....MMO CD 6841 $24.98
____ Standards for Trumpet, vol. 2:
  Pure Imagination (Bob Zottola).......................MMO CD 6842 $24.98
____ Standards for Trumpet, vol. 3 (Bob Zottola) ....MMO CD 6843 $24.98
____ Standards for Trumpet, vol. 4: Stardust (Bob Zottola) ......MMO CD 6844 $24.98
____ Standards for Trumpet, vol. 5 (Bob Zottola) ....MMO CD 6845 $24.98
____ Standards for Trumpet, vol. 6:
  In the Wee Small Hours (Bob Zottola) ....MMO CD 6846 $24.98
____ Studio City.......................MMO CD 2022 $19.98
____ Sweet Sixteen Sax Duets (Hal McCusick) ....MMO CD 4235 $19.98
____ Swing with a Band ....MMO CD 4229 $19.98
____ Take One (minus Lead Tenor Saxophone).......................MMO CD 2012 $19.98
____ Tenor Jazz Jam ....MMO CD 4214 $19.98
____ The Swing Era: Munich Brass ....MMO CD 4220 $19.98
____ Chicago-Style Jam Session ....MMO CD 4218 $19.98
____ Adventures in N.Y. & Chicago Jazz ....MMO CD 4219 $19.98
____ 20 Dixieland Classics ....MMO CD 4207 $24.98
____ Two Much! 16 Tenor Duets for Saxophone
  (Hal McCusick) ....MMO CD 4234 $19.98
____ When Jazz Was Young ....MMO CD 3829 $19.98

Latin Classics
____ JOBIM Brazilian Bossa Novas w/Strings ....MMO CD 3871 $24.98
____ JOBIM Brazilian Bossa Novas w/Strings ....MMO CD 4206 $29.98

Student Series
____ Easy Jazz Duets 2 Tnr Saxes/Rhythm Sec ....MMO CD 4203 $19.98
____ Easy Tenor Sax Solos: v. I ....MMO CD 4201 $19.98
____ Easy Tenor Sax Solos: v. II ....MMO CD 4202 $19.98
____ Take a Chorus ....MMO CD 7008 $19.98
____ Twelve Classic Jazz Standards ....MMO CD 7010 $19.98
____ Twelve More Classic Jazz Standards ....MMO CD 7011 $19.98

ALL PRICES SUBJECT TO CHANGE

SOLO E♭ ALTO SAXOPHONE

I'm In The Mood For Love

Words and Music by Jimmy McHugh
and Dorothy Fields

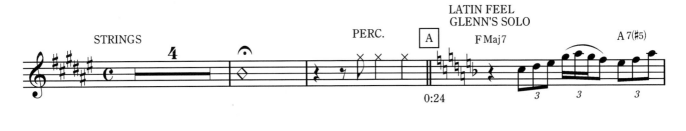

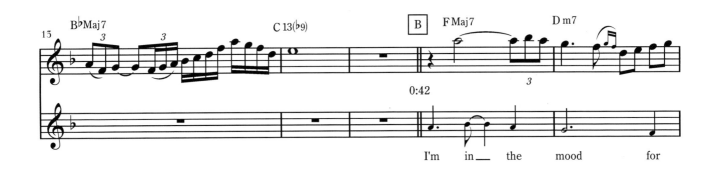

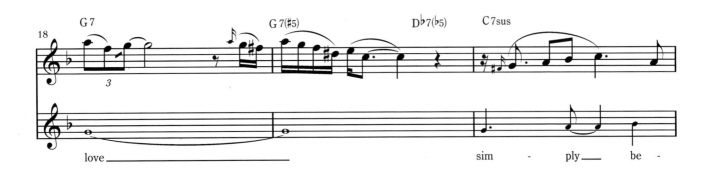

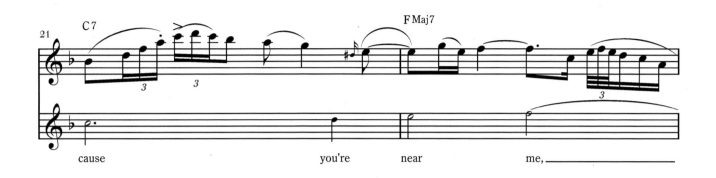

cause you're near me, _____

_____ fun - ny but when you're

near me _____ I'm in __ the mood for

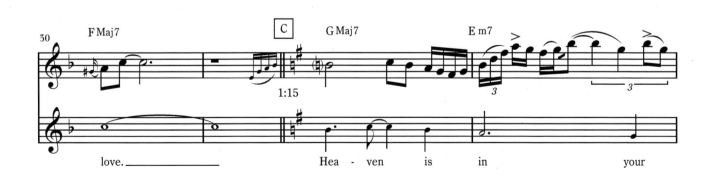

love. _____ Hea - ven is in your

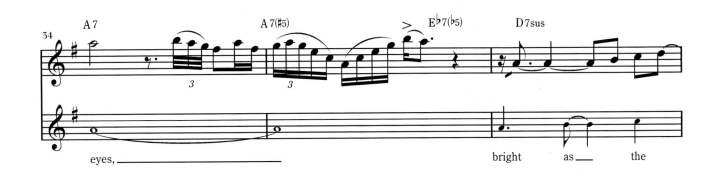

eyes, _____ bright as __ the

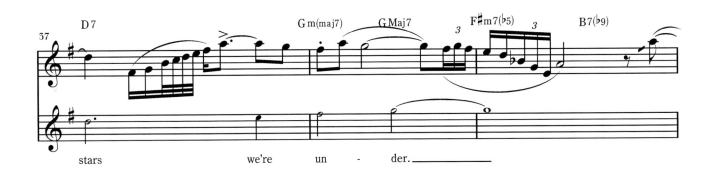

stars we're un - der. _____

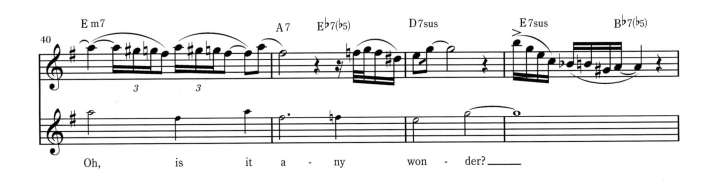

Oh, is it a - ny won - der? _____

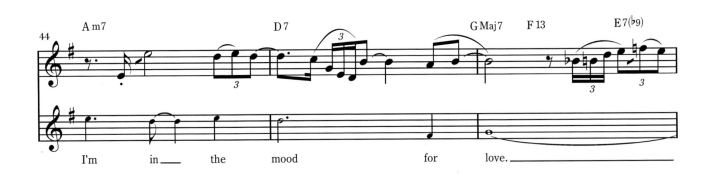

I'm in __ the mood for love. _____

D

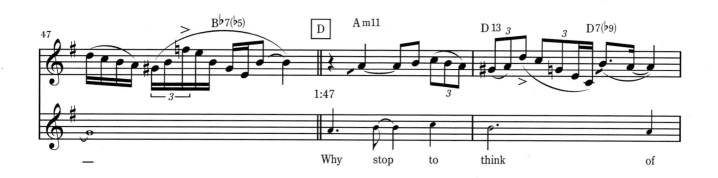

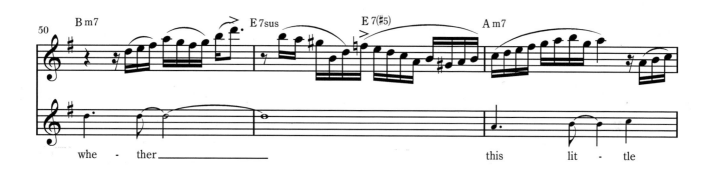

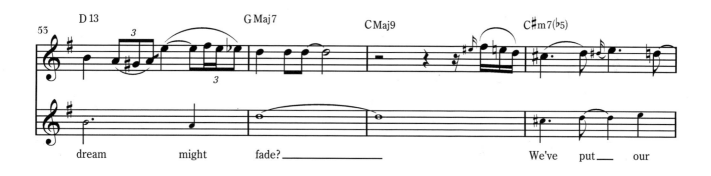

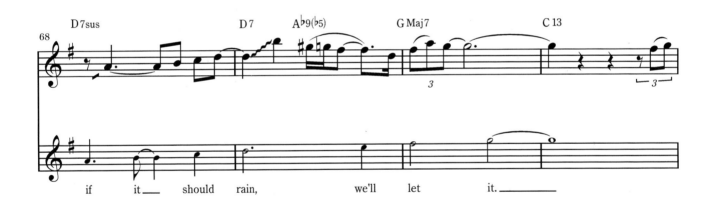

SOLO E♭ ALTO SAXOPHONE

Embraceable You

from Crazy for You
Music and Lyrics by George Gershwin
and Ira Gershwin

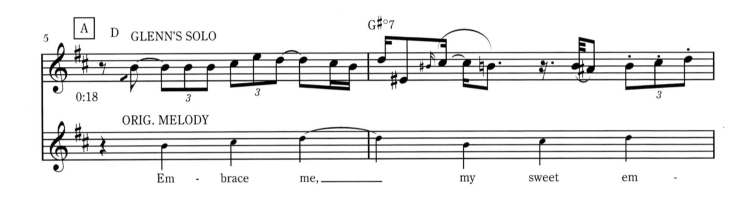

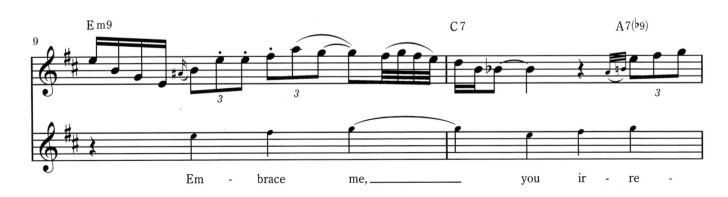

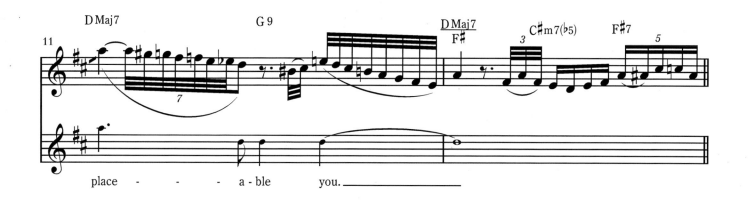

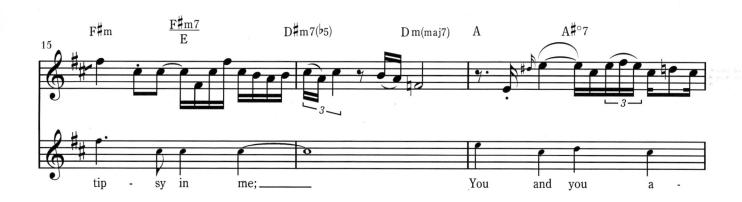

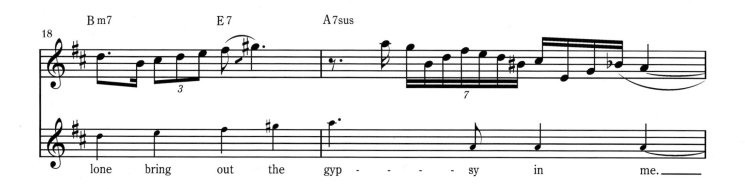

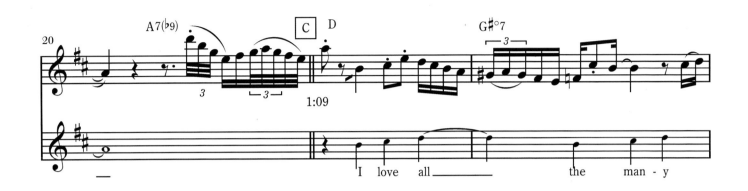

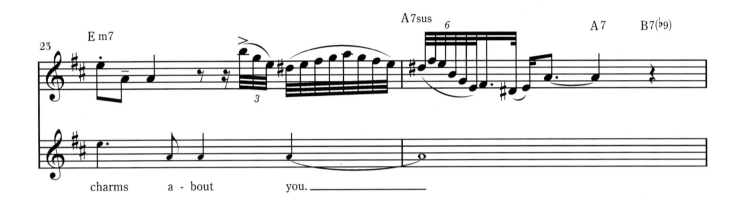

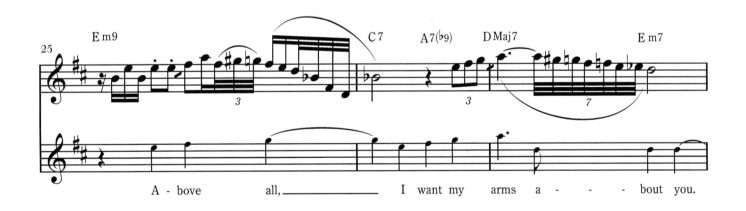

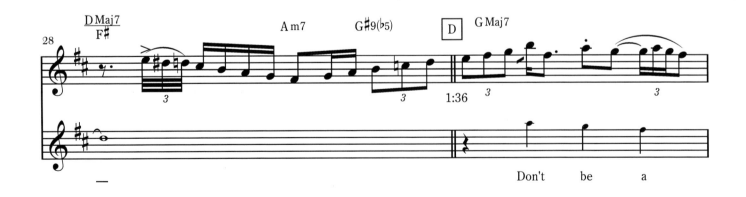

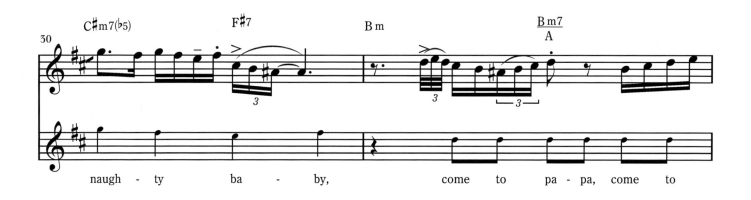

naugh - ty ba - by, come to pa - pa, come to

pa - pa, do. My sweet em - brace - a - ble

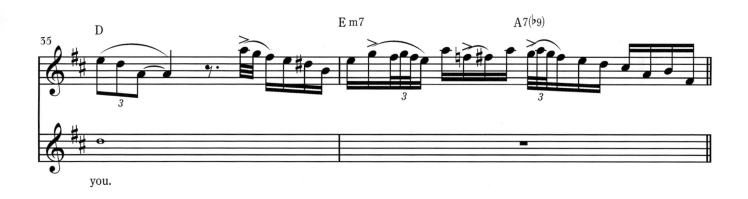

you.

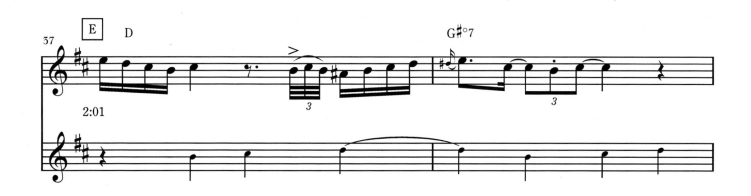

2:01

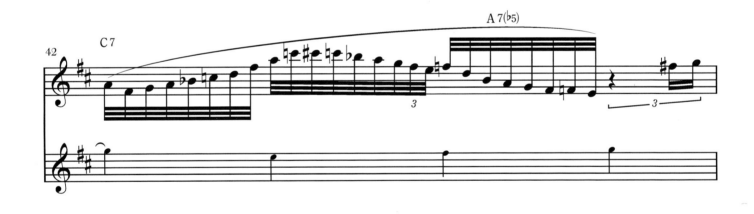

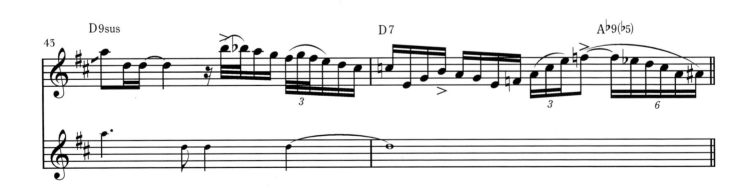

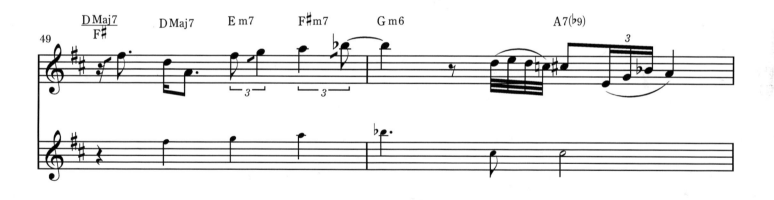

SOLO Eb ALTO SAXOPHONE

Smoke Gets In Your Eyes

from Roberta
Words by Otto Harbach
Music by Jerome Kern

They ____ asked me how I knew my true love was

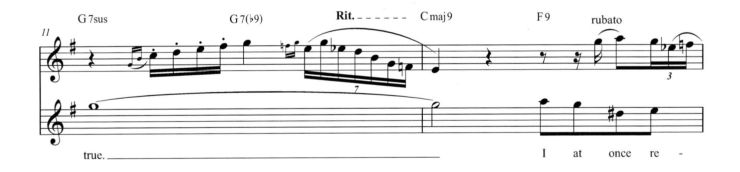

true. ____ I at once re-

plied, some-thing here in-side side can-not be de-

nied.

They said some - day you'll find all who love are

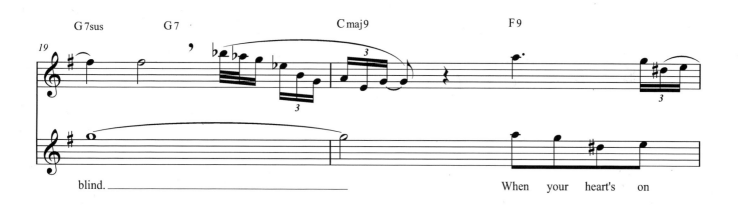

blind. _____ When your heart's on

fire, you must re - al - lize, smoke gets in yours

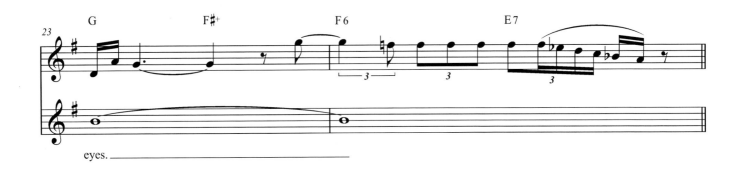

So   I   chafed ____ them   and   I   gay - ly   laughed _____ to   think   they   could

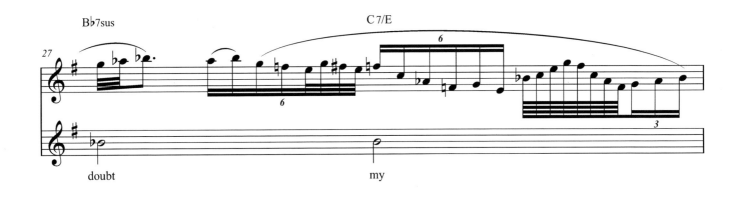

doubt   my

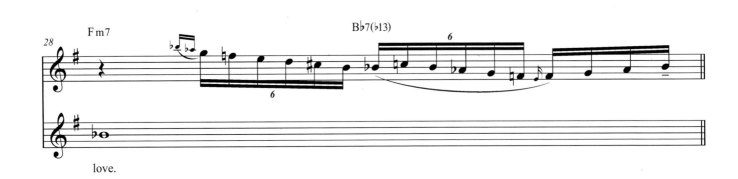

love.

Ebmaj7　　G7(#9)　　Cm9　　Bb9

Yet to-day＿＿＿ my love has gone a - way, ＿＿＿ I am with -

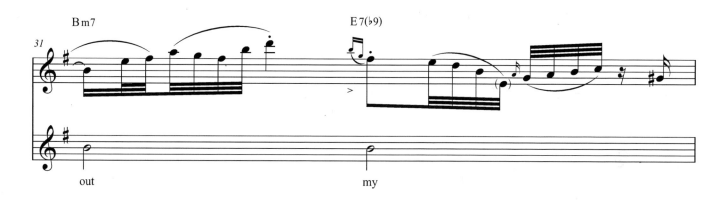

Bm7　　E7(b9)

out　　　　　　　my

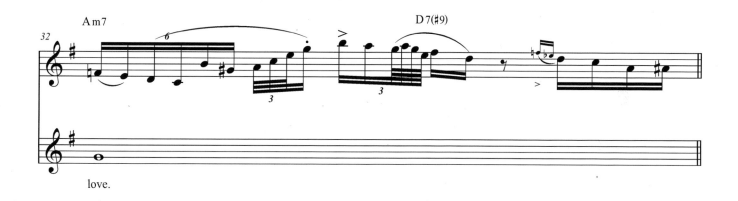

Am7　　D7(#9)

love.

D G　　　Bb°7　　　Am7　　D7(#9)

2:17

Now　　laugh - ing friends de - ride,　　tears I can - not

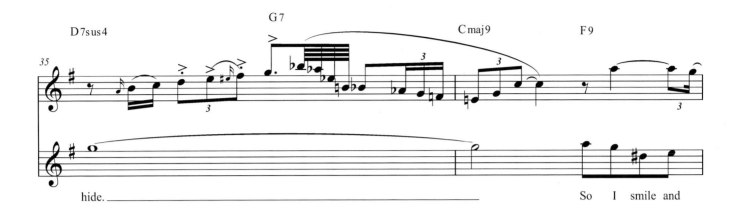

hide. _____ So I smile and

say,   "when a lovely flame   dies,   smoke gets   in yours   eyes. _____

_   So   I   chafed _____ them   and   I

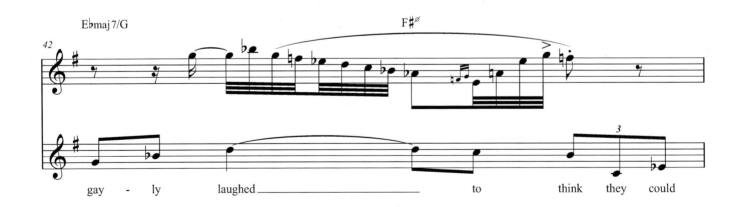

gay - ly   laughed _____ to   think   they   could

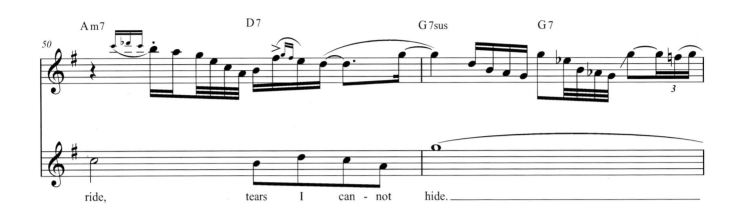

ride,   tears   I   can - not   hide.

__   So   I   smile   and   say,   "when   a   lovely   flame

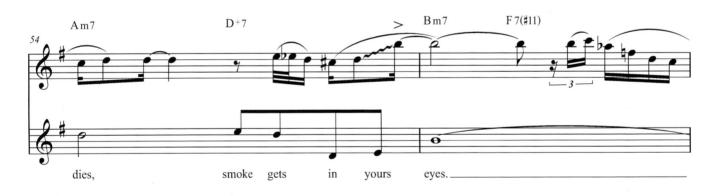

dies,   smoke   gets   in   yours   eyes.

G

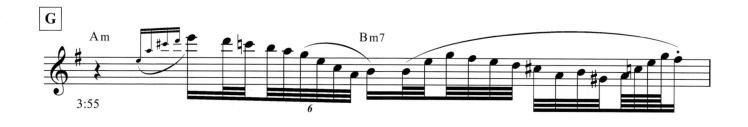

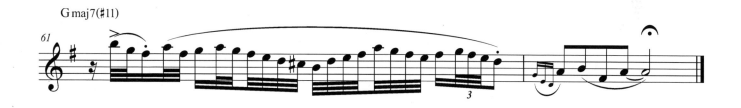

SOLO E♭ ALTO SAXOPHONE

I May Be Wrong

Words by Harry Ruskin
Music by Henry Sullivan

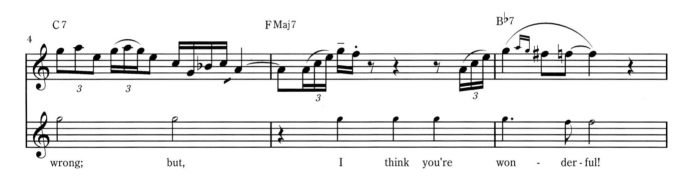

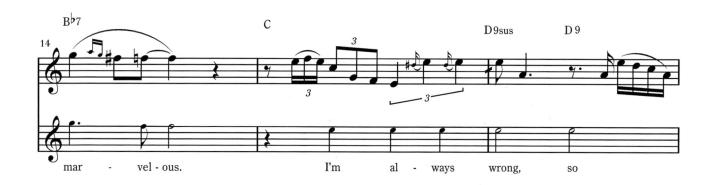

mar - vel - ous. I'm al - ways wrong, so

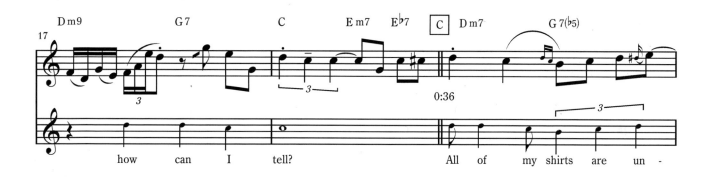

how can I tell? All of my shirts are un -

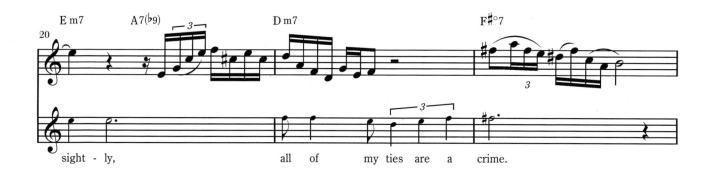

sight - ly, all of my ties are a crime.

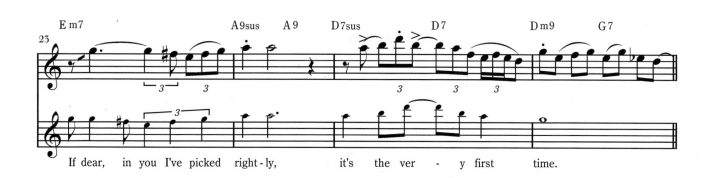

If dear, in you I've picked right - ly, it's the ver - y first time.

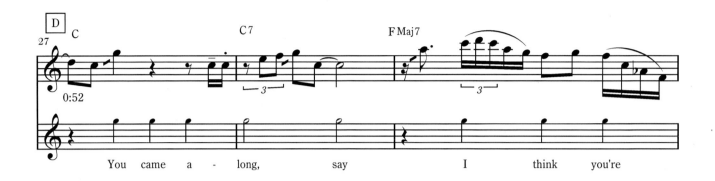

You came a - long, say I think you're

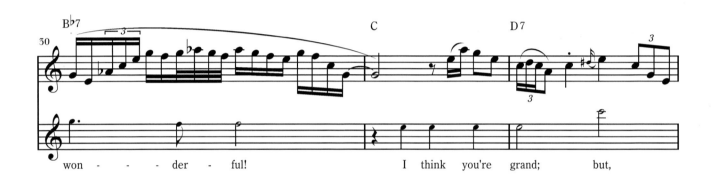

won - - - der - ful! I think you're grand; but,

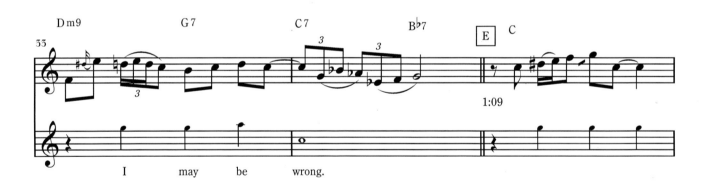

I may be wrong.

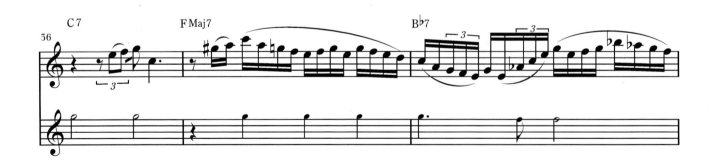

OTHER RECORDINGS BY GLENN ZOTTOLA

MMO CD 12221 Too Marvelous For Words
Glenn Zottola Standards for Tenor Sax

In his career, Glenn Zottola has been best known as a brilliant and swinging trumpeter who occasionally doubles effectively on Alto Sax. But on this special project, he is heard as a talented tenor saxophonist who draws on the sounds and styles of Lester Young and Coleman Hawkins, finding his own voice somewhere in between. Glenn sounds quite at home playing with the vintage rhythm sections yet give the music his own twist and never tries to just merely copy or recreate the past. The icing on the cake is the fact that we've transposed Glenn's every note enabling the at-home player to study and emulate these improvised solos. The sheet music also contains the original melody line of these classic standards, plus chords and an alto sax part, so that both Bb and Eb saxes can play this album with equal enjoyment. The songs in this album are among the greatest standards of our times and the three rhythm sections feature truly all-star legendary players of the first rank in jazz The rhythm sections sprinkled with such names, as Oscar Pettiford, Kenny Clarke, Barry Galbraith, Jimmy Rainey, Don Abney and Milt Hinton attests to the legendary stature of your accompanying players. The songs, all standards, familiar to all players. It never gets this good!

Too Marvelous For Words • Body and Soul • Oh, Lady Be Good • Embraceable You • Three Little Words • Poor Butterfly • Sometimes I'm Happy • You Go To My Head • When Your Lover Has Gone • Fine and Dandy

MMO CD 12222 Glenn Zottola-I Got Rhythm
Standards for Tenor Sax, Vol. 2

This second album in the series, again features Glenn Zottola on tenor sax performing some of the greatest standards of the 20th century with three all-star rhythm sections. As on MMO 12221, the exact performances have been transcribed to enable the at-home player to study and emulate these solos, gaining a better understanding of the music. As before, the printed music allows for use by an alto sax, with original melody line, and lyrics provided as well as chords. The rhythm sections sprinkled with such names, as Oscar Pettiford, Kenny Clarke, Barry Galbraith, Jimmy Rainey, Don Abney and Milt Hinton attests to the legendary stature of your accompanying players. The songs, all standards, familiar to all players. It never gets this good!

Jeepers Creepers • I Only Have Eyes for You • April in Paris • Just One of Those Things • I May Be Wrong • Dont Take Your Love From Me • What is This Thing Called Love • The Man I Love • Lover Come Back To Me • My Heart Stood Still • I Got Rhythm

CJ 2 Jazz Titans - The Classic Jazz Trio

Glenn Zottola, *trumpet & alto sax;* Mark Shane, *piano & vocals;* Mark Maniatt, *drums*
This album is aptly titled Jazz Titans as it features two extraordinary performers in a classic Armstrong and Hines mode, with a bit of Fats thrown in for good measure.

Jubilee • These Foolish Things • • Yardbird Suite • There Is No Greater Love • I Can't Believe That You're In Love With Me • Whispers In The Dark • Polka Dots And Moonbeams • 2:19 Blues • After You've Gone • If I Had You • Spring Cleaning • Soon • The Love Nest • Memories Of You • Whispering • Whispers In The Dark

CJ 4 The Bechet Legacy *(2 CD Set)*
Bob Wilber - Glenn Zottola • Birch Hall Concerts Live

In 1981 Lancaster, England before a packed house, the Bechet Legacy came to play. Both evenings were recorded live! Led by Bob Wilber, Soprano Sax and Clarinet, co-led by Glenn Zottola on trumpet, the tandem front line presented Bechet, Ellington and Armstrong classics in a manner not equalled nor surpassed since. These two concerts were put to tape in front of a full house and you're in the audience. Over two hours of classic jazz!! The all-star band included Mark Shane, on piano, Butch Miles, a former Basie drummer, Mike Peters on guitar and Len Skeat, one of England's finest bassists. Vocals by Pug Horton.

Disc 1: *Oh, Lady Be Good • Down In Honky Tonk Town • Coal Cart Blues • Egyptian Fantasy • Lazy Blues • Summertime • The Mooche • Daydream • Si Tu Vois Ma Mere • Dans Le Reu D'Antibes • I Keep Calling Your Name • Sweet Lorraine*

Disc 2: *I Let A Song Go Out Of My Heart • China Boy • I Got It Bad And That Ain't Good • Just One Of Those Things • Polka Dot Stomp • Happiness Is Just A Thing Call Joe • Dear Old Southland • Promenade Aux Champs-Elysees • Georgia Cabin • Memories of You • Swing That Music*

SOLO E♭ ALTO SAXOPHONE

Three Little Words

from the Motion Picture Check and Double Check
Lyrics by Bert Kalmar
Music by Harry Ruby

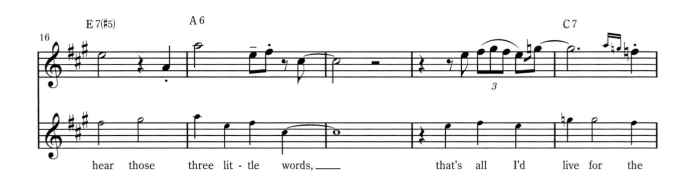

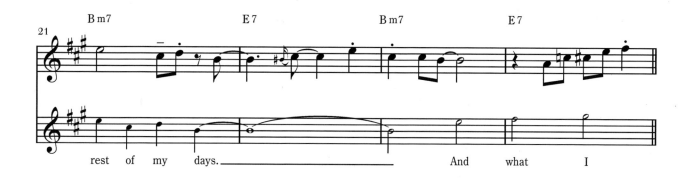

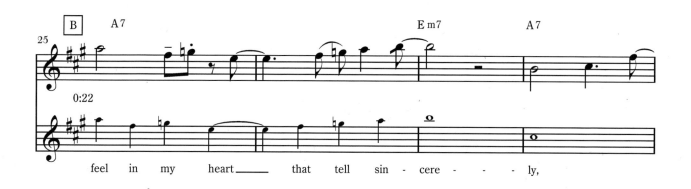

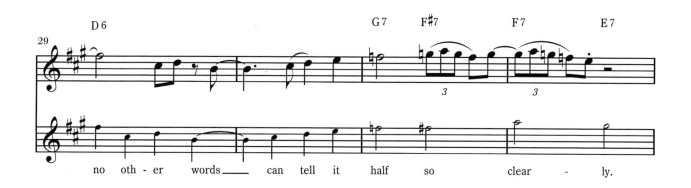

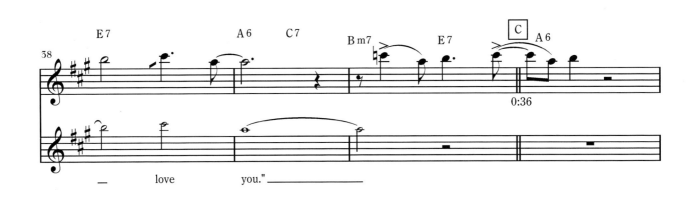

love you." _____

MMO 12223

2:05

MUSIC MINUS ONE
50 Executive Boulevard
Elmsford, New York 10523-1325
800-669-7464 (US) • 914-592-1188 (International)

www.musicminusone.com
e-mail: info@musicminusone.com

MMO 12223

ISBN 1-59615-841-2